Look and Find®

publications international, ltd.

D0557090

When Princess Anna first discovers her sister Elsa's magical power, she thinks it's wonderful! Look around this winter wonderland to find these things the two sisters made, thanks to Princess Elsa's icy magic:

this igloo

snow angel

this flurry of snow

this sledding hill

pyramid of snowballs

Olaf the snowman

After Elsa accidentally puts a white streak in Anna's hair, the king worries she may hurt her little sister. Elsa decides to stay away from Anna to keep her safe. But Anna doesn't know this and can't understand why Elsa won't play with her anymore. Look around for these things that Anna would like to share with her sister:

ice cream cones

dollhouse

jump rope

chess game

wish bone

these dolls

People from all over the world have come to Arendelle to attend Elsa's coronation. Find the charming Prince Hans of the Southern Isles as well as these other visitors:

Once the townspeople see Elsa's icy magic, they become frightened. Afraid she'll hurt someone with her powers, Elsa runs from the castle. As she flees, look around the courtyard for these frozen creations:

this flag

icy lantern

this fountain

this topiary

this topiary

this stone

Anna climbs up the mountain to find her sister, but soon she realizes that she needs help. A mountain man named Kristoff seems to have the know-how. Search Oaken's Trading Post to find these supplies that might help, too:

this sweater

this grappling hook

flint

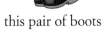
this pair of boots

rope

telescope

this ice axe

Kristoff agrees to help Anna, but before long he wonders whether that was such a good idea! While they flee from the wolves, look for Kristoff's scattered belongings:

scorched blanket

broken lute

sweater

sock

hat

mitten

Anna finally finds her sister. But when Anna asks Elsa to come home, Elsa says she can't. She doesn't want to go back to Arendelle where the people will never accept her for who she is. As Elsa creates a snowman named Marshmallow, look for these other icy items she has made:

Summer has finally returned to Arendelle! To thank Kristoff for helping her, Anna gives him a brand-new sled and supplies. She even remembered to buy carrots for Sven! Look around town for these other things that Sven might need:

halter

water bucket

apple

snow goggles

blanket

snowshoes

Return to the two young sisters playing in the snow to find these items that could decorate a snowman:

carrot for nose

this lump of coal

branch for arm

these mittens

big button

this winter hat

Skip back to the scenes of the sisters growing up and search for these things that Anna enjoys solo:

knitting needles

guitar

yo-yo

book

tricycle

swing

Arendelle's visitors did not travel light! Go back to the docks to find these supplies:

this crate of potatoes

this crate of apples

wheel of cheese

sack of flour

bale of hay

barrel of pickled herring

As Elsa flees Arendelle, look for these frightened townspeople:

Go back to Oaken's Trading Post to find these troll souvenirs that are for sale:

Run back to the wolves and identify these animal tracks in the snow:

bear

moose

arctic fox

musk ox

beaver

horse

Return to Elsa's dazzling ice palace to find these unique ice creations:

Search the streets of Arendelle to find these six pairs of sisters enjoying the summer sun: